T0353785

Live for Each Day

PERSONAL POETRY COLLECTION

Rick B. Jimenez

WestBow Press books may be ordered through booksellers or by contacting:

WestBow Press
A Division of Thomas Nelson & Zondervan
1663 Liberty Drive
Bloomington, IN 47403
www.westbowpress.com
844-714-3454

ISBN: 979-8-3850-2985-3 (sc)
ISBN: 979-8-3850-3102-3 (hc)
ISBN: 979-8-3850-2984-6 (e)

Library of Congress Control Number: 2024914881

Print information available on the last page.

WestBow Press rev. date: 8/1/2024

WESTBOW
PRESS®
A DIVISION OF THOMAS NELSON
& ZONDERVAN

Live for Each Day

A book of Poetry

Introduction

I dedicate this book of poems to Vanessa, my daughter, a
special part of me, a little piece of me. I love you kiddo.
And to my Mom, Maria, who has always been there for me.
You have been the lighthouse of faith, hope and strength
in my life, to you I a dedicate "Dear Friend of mine".
I love you both with all my heart.

I believe that God has given me this talent to write. I was
inspired to write poetry because I learned that my father and
uncle were poetic with their words and the letters they wrote.

I hope that these poems will be an encouragement
for you and everyone who reads them.

Table of Contents

Note/Message

Love at first sight

The first time I saw you, wow, what a sight to see,
was my first reaction when I first noticed you.

For I was captivated by your beauty, and your
gorgeous smile. And it was your beautiful
romantic eyes, that I was surrendered to see.

Time seemed to stop for a moment for me, as I admired your
beauty and the radiance and glory of your beautiful hair.

I knew that very moment what I felt in my heart, that
I had fallen in love, for it was love at first sight.

You are always on my mind and in my heart

As I go about my day, thoughts of you come to mind. And I begin to wonder – how wonderful it would be to have you in my life.

Time seems to pass me by so quickly, and I continue to hold you deep within my heart. For I wait patiently for the moment that you will allow me into your life.

Oh what a day that will be, and the happiness it will bring to my life, because you are always on my mind and in my heart.

You are my inspiration

As I think about my motivation and need to succeed,
I think about you and my desire to see you achieve
excellence and continue to move ahead.

Always remember to follow your dreams and never give
up and settle for less, because life's true success is the
satisfaction and contentment in doing what you love best.

In your weakest moments of doubt and despair, remember to
have faith in God and believe in yourself, and always remember
that you are my inspiration, and I will always be there, like the
wind beneath your wings to always help you move a head.

Dear friend of mine

God has placed you in my path to help brighten
up my days and bring sunshine to my life.

You've encouraged me when I needed it most, and
have been my friend in my loneliest times.

You have helped me to believe and have faith that everything
would be alright. You have walked with me and helped
carry the burdens that were so weighing me down.

For all you have done to help brighten up my
life, I am thankful to God, to be blessed with
your friendship, dear friend of mine.

Live for each day

Live each day like it's your last.
Tell your loved ones that you love them, and show them your
affection with tender hearted words, hugs, kisses, and especially
your actions. Don't wait for tomorrow, for tomorrow isn't
promised and you may miss the chance to see them once again.

Don't let each day go by neglecting the only
chance that you may have, to make the best of
yourself and the opportunities you have.

So don't let each day pass like the wind that blows by, instead
be thankful to God and live each day like it's your last.

Challenge yourself to succeed

Challenge yourself to succeed and don't let your past
failures defeat you; instead, decide to conquer them with
faith, hope, and determination for a better tomorrow,
because you refuse to be defeated by failure.

You're failures will just become your stepping stones
that will lead you to the platoes of your success.

And once you achieve any level of success, take the time to
help others along the way who may be struggling to get ahead.

Life's greatest joys will not be in what you can achieve for
yourself. Your greatest joys will come from your ability to
be able to help others and make a difference in someone
else's life, when you challenge yourself to succeed.

True beauty which shines from within

You're beauty, is like the radiance of a full moon, and like the glow of the brightest star which shines in the soft quiet night sky. It's like the first gleam of dawn which shines ever brighter and fills me up with joy the moment I look at you.

As I look into your heart, I can see that you're gorgeous, tender-hearted, loving and kind. Your beauty is like a true beauty that shines from within, which starts at the heart where Jesus lives.

Make a difference in the life of a child

Whether you live near or far, make a difference in the
life of a child. It doesn't take much, but a portion of
our time, and our commitment and dedication to break
away from the business of life and spend quality time.

When we take time to spend time, we invest time
in the life of a child in a positive way. And the
memories created will have lasting effects in that
child you decided to spend time with today.

The difference you can make may have ripple
effects on future generations to come, if you decide
to make a difference in the life of a child.

Time
The most valuable gift we were given

Not one second that goes by is not counted, not one minute
that passes that will be wasted if time is something we treasure.

Don't waste your time on senseless things that will rob
you of your precious time, instead think and analyze
if the thing to do is really worth your time.

Who can give you back a minute of you time, or turn
the clock back one minute day or night. For seconds
will quickly turn turn minutes, and minutes into hours,
and hours to days which are accompanied by nights.

The days will soon turn into weeks, and weeks to
months and months to years of your precious life.

Try to avoid having regrets later in life by making the most out of your time, by dedicating most of your time to the things which matter most and minimize wasting your time on those things which matter least.

If I have the chance to tell you that I love you

If I have a chance to tell you that I love you, I will show you. I will open up my heart and reveal to you just how special you are to me. I will express my love for you in ways that will make you feel treasured and appreciated, honored and respected.

I will buy you roses, just because. I will play your favorite song just to make you smile. I will cheer you up when you're feeling down. I will learn to sing a new song so I can entertain your heart. I will give the greatest importance to every detail of significance that matters in your life.

There's no end to the things that I will do and the infinite ways I will express my love for you. If I have the chance to tell you that I love you, I will show you.

God's love is eternal, forgiving and free

God's love is different, try him and you will see,
that God's love is eternal, forgiving and free.

For God loved you so much, that he sent his only son
Jesus, to die on the cross and pay for your sins.

If you give your heart to Jesus and allow him to come in, He
will be your Lord and Savior, Counselor, Protector and Friend.

He will give you a new life to live as you are born again.
Born not of flesh and blood but of your spirit within. For by
the precious blood of Jesus – God will wash away your sins.

If God is knocking on the door of your heart
today and you receive him you will see, that
God's love is eternal, forgiving and free.

A good friendship is like a strong cord of strands

A friendship is like a cord of strands, which begins as a single strand. As the relationship grows, through love, compassion, bonding and fellowship, more strands are added and weaved together into a cord of strands.

Through nurture, appreciation, respect, and the sharing of burdens, a friendship is strengthened.

On the other hand, bitterness, anger, jealousy and ill will, is like rust which decays and ruins the strands – destroying the friendship that you once had.

A word of advice from my own experience, choose your friends wisely – for true friends are few, and you will discover in time, that when your resources are low, and you're going through hard times, your true friends will stay with you to see you through to the end like a strong cord of strands.

Back to the past

If I could go back to the past, I would visit
the moments that you needed me most. Those
moments of sadness, those moments of tears, and
the moments you faced your greatest fears.

I would hug and embrace you like a good caring
dad. I would wipe away your tears and give you a
hope for tomorrow and better days near. I would
protect, guide you, and take away your fears.

I would give you encouragement to help
strengthen your faith and help build your self
esteem, so you may believe in your dreams.

If I could go back to the past, I would capture
the moments and cherish the times as I make a
difference to help brighten up your life.

Saying good by

Saying good by to you is not easy to say or do, for
you hold a special place in my heart for you.

You've always been so dear to me, and no words can
fully express, just how much you mean to me.

The special moments that we shared together,
are special memories in time that will remain
forever in my heart and in my mind.

As I take this moment to say my last good by,
I will forever cherish the friendship that we
have, for this was a gift from God.

Never stop dreaming, Never give up

Never stop dreaming, never give up. And always remember to keep your dreams alive every morning when you wake up.

Remember your childhood years, when dreaming of great things or what to become, was uncluttered by negativity and doubtful voices that say it couldn't be done.

There's no limit to what you can do or who you want to become, if you believe in yourself and hold on to your dreams with all your heart.

Just take a moment and close your eyes, and envision your dreams coming to life. Then develop a plan to go after your dreams, and soon you will realize that you can succeed.

I'll see you later my friend

It's not good by or farewell, I'll see you later my
friend, because I know I will see you again.

It comforts me to know that your soul is now in heaven
in the presence of the Lord. Free of suffering from
sorrow and life's ills and pains, surrounded by God's
holy angels and others who have gone ahead.

While I continue to live the life, God has destined
me to live, you'll continue to live in my heart
and my mind until the day I see you again.

Thank you for your friendship

You're friendship has meant so much to me. You have inspired me to do great things and to have a greater belief in me.

You have complimented my life in many ways, by the sharing of your positive thoughts and your godly views on life.

Thank you for your friendship, and for sharing your wonderful life with me dear friend. For by being the good friend you are to me today, you have also shown me how to be a good friend to others on the way.

Near the river stream

The steady flow of water is soothing and refreshing to my soul

There as I sit by the river, I reflect on good old times, and visualize as I close my eyes of those memorable moments of fun and joyous times, enjoying the refreshing water that flows by.

I can hear the laughter as I remember of those fun and memorable moments in time. Oh how I long to revisit the past, and relive those fun and memorable moments we once had.

There by the river I sit, hearing the sound of the water as I close my eyes, and imagine those fun and memorable moments near the river stream water that flows by.

Faith that grows

Like the roots of a tree grow in search of water in times of scarcity and drought. So does my faith grow during times of adversity, trials, and when my resources run low.

I cannot falter, I can't give up, I have to keep going, because my hope is in Christ and He knows all about my life.

As I make it through my struggles and get past a circumstance, I see my faith growing stronger than it was.

Faith that grows, is the faith that continually hopes and never gives up, and instead says a prayer for a little help from above.

Lord let me be your hands and feet

Lord let me be your hands and feet, so I may visit
and feed those who are hungry and in need.

Lord give me eyes to see and ears to hear, the cries of
all those who hope to see and hear you near, so I may
share of your great love and intercede on their behalf.

Lord help me live a blameless life, so I may
give you glory by the way I live my life.

Lord let me be what you want me to be, and in all
I become, Lord let me be your hands and feet.

If I could wish upon a star

As the evening ends and the night begins and I
begin to miss you once again, I often look up at
the sky and search to find the brightest star.

As I gaze up at the star and I wonder how you are, I also
hope you see it too whenever you miss me as I miss you.

If I could wish upon a star, I'd wish for us to be
closer than we are. We could then both look up at the
sky and appreciate the beauty of the night, without
missing each other so often times at night.

Success will be my reward

In my search to have success, I must first enjoy
my life and appreciate all I already have.

I should strive on constant improvement, I should
always be under control. I should be committed to
quality, and work on diminishing errors as I go.

If I commit myself to excellence in all I do,
then success will be my reward.

True friends

God has blessed me with true friends that have
stood the test of time. I've sown love into their
hearts, and they have enriched my life.

True friends that won't leave me when I'm going through
the trials and storms of life, are the ones that help
encourage me when I'm going through tough times.

As I celebrate the happy moments in my life, I especially
want my closest friends to be there by my side, those
whose true friendship have made an impact on my life.

To be wise

If you want to be wise, then listen to good advise.

Advise from a godly friend that makes
good sense, may be wise to accept.

From the experience of others and the lessons they have
learned, sound judgment is learned and wisdom is earned.

The ultimate wisdom is found in God's word, inspired
by God's Holy Spirit, then written in books.

If you want to be wise, then seek godly advise. And sooner
or later you'll know what is right. For discernment and good
judgment are traits of the wise, who always seek godly advise.

Find a reason to celebrate

Life is precious – no time to spare, make time
to celebrate with those you love and care.

Life is too short for holding grudges and keeping
distance for hard feelings and misunderstandings,
forgive the wrong doing. So you'll find joy in your
heart and help restore the relationship you once had.

Just take the initiative and show that you care, and find a
special reason to celebrate with those you love and care.

On my way

A time to say good by is what I feel today. It's a
decision to part and be on my way, in search to find,
what God has in mind for my journey today.

It's a special feeling, It's an inspiring moment, when
I feel that I'm done with a certain calling.

Life has it's journeys and short stays along the way, and
sometimes I feel when it's time to move on and be on my way.

If I depart

If I depart from your life, remember this, I am leaving, but not leaving you. I'll be gone, but not for long, for the special memories will live on in your heart for many years to come.

As the seasons change and you stop for a moment, feeling sad as you think about the life that we once had, remember the special moments that we once shared and treasured, you'll find comfort and smile and feel better.

Go on live your life, enjoying every moment that passes by. For what matters most are the memories that are treasured and cherished and kept close to your heart.

For love to last

For love to last, it must be pure and sincere. It must
be mutual and well received. And most of all, it
must be true, it must be real to pass the test of time
and the challenges and trials that life brings on.

Because pride, rejection, and loss of affection may
cause the feeling of love to fade away and die.

For love to last and pass the test of time and challenges
of life, it must be a decision to choose to love for all
the right reasons, despise all the bad seasons.

Don't let time slip on by

Find your passion live your dream, don't let time slip on by. It slips away just like the night, then when you awake you realize that another day has passed you by. You'll then be left with much regret about the things you could have done, or accomplishments you could have made.

Time is golden, time is precious, the most valuable asset you possess. Don't let it slip on by, don't let it slip away, by doing senseless things or with people who don't care. Unless for a worthy cause or with people that you love and care, be wise with your time, don't let it slip on by.

If you want your life to be the way you've always
dreamed of, then be efficient with your time,
don't let it slip on by, don't let it slip away.

Spend all the time you can on setting goals and
meeting them, for they'll each help you get one
step closer to accomplishing your dreams.

One day you may reflect on your past life and the memories
that you've made, weather good or bad will depend on the
things you did today, and on how you spent your days.

Love will find a way

When you're feeling lonely and sad because you've been hurt
by someone so dear to your heart, love will find a way

When that special someone whose been so close
to your heart, stops communicating and you
don't understand why, love them anyway.

If you have to look for them because you care so much.
Have faith in God, and ask for His help to restore the
great friendship you once had. Love will find a way.

Success & Failure

Success is a journey, not a destination.
Failure is full of disappointments and many good lessons.

If I'm to succeed, I must never give up or give
in to the disappointments life brings.

If I should stumble and fail, I will turn to God,
who will lift me up and make me strong.

Failure is an occurrence, not a state of mind.
There's always hope for anyone who reaches
out in faith for help and doesn't give up.

Worker of the Harvest

Lord use my life, to work the harvest of the souls
you have called to salvation and eternal life.

Help me to also be an encouragement to anyone called and
chosen to work the harvest field as I have been chosen.

I will magnify your love and glorify your name, as you
ignite the light of my life through the holy spirit, to shine
bright in the dark paths and valleys of peoples lives.

Social Distance

It's a difficult time we're in, it's a matter of life,
we must keep social distance to stay alive.

It's a dangerous disease that's attacking out lives, it's
called Covid-19 and there's no vaccine to fight it.
We must stay in our homes, It's been ordered by government.
It's for the best for our families and the survival of our society.
This will help slow the spread of this terrible virus, and
will help minimize the deaths that this disease is causing.

Let's keep working together, let's keep doing
what's right, so we help win the fight.

Let's keep social distance – it's a small sacrifice. It'll help
do our part while the find a vaccine to help fight it. Some
day we'll look back and reflect on this moment, when the
whole world got caught by surprise with this terrible virus.

A bite your size

On a cold and misty morning said the frog to the fly, "it seems like a very nice morning for a bite just your size mr fly."

Then the fly says to the frog, "yes it is mr. frog, but it's also just as nice a day for a cat to catch a bite just your size."

Then the frog says to the fly, "on second thought mr. fly, it's just as nice of a day for us to enjoy this misty morning just as friends you and I.

Follow your Dream

If you wake up one morning from dreaming what you'd love to be or do and you wish with all your heart for this to be a reality in your life, just follow your dream.

When the going gets tough and doubt starts to settle in because of difficulties and challenges which block the road ahead, just close your eyes and imagine that you're already there and just follow your dream.

Once you're back on track and everything starts to go well, don't get comfortable there, remember to keep going toward the road ahead and do all to prepare to reach your goal and just follow your dream.

You're dream will reward you once it becomes a reality in your life. You'll enjoy the fruits of your labor and be satisfied from within by bringing to life the dream you kept alive.

So just follow your dream and never give up and
do all to prepare and strive to get ahead, for at just
the right moment the dream you wished with all
your heart will become a reality in your life.

Don't give up

Although times are bad and you're
feeling quite sad, don't give up.

Even though you've lost that special someone in
your life and you're feeling like the whole world
has come down on you and you're having trouble
keeping your head up, even then, don't give up.

When you're feeling sad and lonely and need someone
to love and comfort you, just look around to your family
and friends and you'll find the comfort and love to help
you carry on, but just remember, don't give up.

And when you miss that special someone and need
their love, comfort and council, just look up, and you're
heavenly father will be there waiting to embrace you,
comfort, council and fill all the voids in your heart.

Printed in the United States
by Baker & Taylor Publisher Services